For over 30 years, Tom Parks traveled the highways and byways of South Carolina and often took photos of scenes that reflected for him the passage of time and place: the state of things in terms of where it has been, where it is now, and where it is going. Now retired and living elsewhere, he leaves this bittersweet record of his thoughts and insights from his years in the State Department of Education, and Professor and Associate Dean at Clemson University. He holds four degrees in English, including a Ph.D. from Vanderbilt University.

Tom Parks

GOODBYE TO A STATE

A TOUR OF SOUTH CAROLINA IN PHOTOGRAPHY AND POETRY

AUSTIN MACAULEY PUBLISHERS™
LONDON • CAMBRIDGE • NEW YORK • SHARJAH

Ordering Information:
Quantity sales: special discounts are available on quantity purchases by corporations, associations, and others. For details, contact the publisher at the address below.

Publisher's Cataloging-in-Publication data
Parks, Tom
Goodbye to a State

ISBN 9781645751335 (Paperback)
ISBN 9781645751328 (Hardback)
ISBN 9781645751342 (ePub e-book)

Library of Congress Control Number: 2020908337

www.austinmacauley.com/us

First Published (2020)
Austin Macauley Publishers LLC
40 Wall Street, 28th Floor
New York, NY 10005
USA

mail-usa@austinmacauley.com
+1 (646) 5125767

Table of Contents

Prologue: From the Mountains to the Sea

A million motes of circumstance
Sit on the throne to which you bow
And if you read me, I am one
Among them. You may curtsy now.
Your countenance to me is moot
I am untouched and play my part
So infinitesimal a spark
That touched you now and added to
Your sum in cold magnetic ways
An algorithm gone agape
At universes filled in you
Wherein you find me circling there
A part of your equation now
And, thus, approach you circumspect
To lead my tour into your state.
While I continue on my way
To circling circumstance and death
I fashion prayers that you may live
My only hope to reign again.
So I am born in breasted hills
Your soft and malleable milk

Gives succor to a rivulet
To green the grass and soak a marsh
Then down the sloping hills I write
With watered pen a creek in birth
In league with rain, I score the earth
And babble on about the sea
Known only to me now in myth
And pause into a deepening flow
To form your lakes and cleanse your frame
Your swollen belly washed in blood
At length I find your brush and roots
And spray a riot of wild seed
In colors, patterns, shapes, and styles
To bloom in natural pulchritude
And catch your eye and slow your play
I stand in reverence of trees
To shade you as your old gods burn

And fill my cooling pools with fish
And crawfish mines and turtle logs
Then snake my arrows at your heart
And watch you age and leave your farms
And pastures manicured and mute
To children thirsting for cement
And bridges to a dryer place
From you and yours and all you were
To others come to take your place
Beneath which I cut clean a path
To separate both time and place
A hint of salt now on my lips
I sense once more this *déjà vu*

And know in passing I have known
Your burning sleep, your frozen face

Thus on my way to be the tide
I dream of your most precious state
And see you now at every turn
At work and worship, bowing down
Before your boxed assorted gods
And watch you nod and curl to sleep
Outside the wisdom of my shade.

Cycle

I have gone ahead
      to prepare a place for you
It awaits, a plot of stolid silence
      the wormy earth not yet turned
The basalt slab to receive your hieroglyph
      still uncut within the quarry
And some unconcerned stonemason
      going about his business this day
Not caring who or what you are
      only that your remains can pay
Birds fly overhead meanwhile
      and clouds come and go
In the seasonal shafts of sun
      knowing you are next
As will their progeny
      when you are gone
And this fine field
      of Whitman's grass
Will require the tiniest bit less
      of soil enrichment
The few salty drops of sorrow
      at your leaving meaningless

To making the balance
        in the strength of fields
Your deeds and your desires
        at the most for me
Will anoint a nodule of nitrogen
        ten thousand years from now
When together we shall flow into each other
        and contemplate resurrection
And then it will be your turn
        perhaps to tell me at length
You have gone ahead
        to prepare a place for me.

Farm scene near Springfield

Belief

That baby was born dead
And they had to take it away from her
She had it named
Had little clothes made for it
Borrowed and begged even hand-me-downs
From those with fewer rooms and walls
Or windows welcoming the light
That followed her throughout the house
Until a mighty mote of fate
Accosted her beside the stair
Gathering bouquets of baby's breath
Months before it was due

Abandoned house, Highway 76

He buried it that very night
In the dark where she wouldn't see
The stars look cold and weak tonight, she said
Maybe I'd better get that extra blanket
To cover up its head
And, passing by the window, saw outside
Her dead daughter at long last dead
And the blank bible
Inside, waiting to be read.

Creation

And they say there is no God
Look on, ye sinners, and despair!
These baptizing waters, these velvet shores
Did not come from nothing
Ten billion drops of water
Fell one at a time in the upcountry
Some on ice, some on heated fields
Soaking into Piedmont foothills
And giving rise to oak and elm
That gorged the air with oxygen
And created a mighty sepulcher
Wherein torrents roared and energy cracked
Echoing among the crags and hills
Then, huddled at his fire
The Mighty Being paused
Heard the sound, saw the fury
And strode from His wooded throne
Throwing up dams, moving cemeteries
And plotting calibrated shores
Planting pines and selling shares
Until these healing waters came forth
Anointing the state of things

All awash in manmade miracle
Then He rested, and now sails His boats
Upon the breaded waters.

Lake Murray at Irmo

Teacher

Restroom duty? Ha!
Misnomer is thy name
At least I know where the *rest* comes from
In the naming of this room
Last May, I found a fetus here
Ten thousand times a thousand times
Its tiny mouth, a slitted gill
Popping for air, a bubble of breath
As it drowned in the blood and urine
Awash in adolescent afterbirth
Of society's ceramic bowl

Why did she have it here?
Excuse me, I forgot
Here's the only home she knows
The distant do-gooders say
So I guess it's all right
If she squats delivery here
To make John feel guilty
Her friends have told him so
The undeniable baby he denied
Lies afloat in the first floor john

So there, Mr. Big Shot
You have hurt her bad
And we hope you worry and suffer
But John goes on
And so does school
The bell ringing me back to third period

Junior high school

I remember when I was twenty-two
Set out to save the world
All aglow in the glow of things
Oh, to hell with it
Open your books to page 22.

Heaven's Gate

It was Jesus, all right
       walking along a dirt road barefooted
Oh, let there be no question
       it was the savior. It was!

With auroras of rich, pastel lights
       pulsating from him, head to foot
And angel music soaring in the air
       as he scuffed along the hot dust
A beatific smile on his alabaster face
       gentle locks cascading to his shoulders
And a white silk robe sashed in gold
       just like on the funeral home fans
Up ahead, the church loomed
       an imposing shade in the sun
Workmen had built it in '34
       cussing when they missed a nail
Drinking beer and oogling
       the freckled country girls
All dead and buried now
       workmen and girls alike
Plopped like cow paddies in this pasture

before the cemetery came
And then one moonless manic night
        four quick and dirty years ago
Norman Potts staggered drunk
        into the pre-fence monuments here
Hunting the marker of his mother
        an unpretentious bit of stone

Country church near Salley

And, finding none, splayed them all around
        at odd angles across the graves
And, cursing the monumental mess
        swaggered out, delivered by his deed
Leaving the lazy minister next morning
        with an easy brimstone sermon
And the deacons with a call
        and cause for the Lord
The fence! The fence! And
        thus saved, worshiped in smug security

Loudly, and with great waving of hands
            they soul-stomped into time and space
Shouting through to salvation
            awash in the warm blood of Jesus
Who padded past now in the powdered dust outside
            shuffling west toward the setting sun
Along the fence and beside the church
            his celestial music and pastels lost
And stopped at Crazy Hattie's house
            a ramshackle shack beside the road
Who blankly gave him the water he begged
            and stared, finger in mouth, as he winged away

Then proclaimed his second coming
            for the rest of her babbling days:
Exactly as we've got him pictured
            on the calendars and velvet paintings
His hair was rich and full of body
            his shampoo a herbal scent
The robe was the finest silk I've seen
            the gold sash pretty as any at Walmart
No, he didn't wear any sandals
            but the hem of his garment
Was sewn low with little tiny cross-stitches
            and kept the dust from his crotch, I figure
His gown sort of cascaded from his shoulders
            in a loose but comfortable curve
And his fingernails were clean
            without hair anywhere but on his head
It was our Jesus, all right
            the true blessed savior

Caught me drinking grape Kool-Aid
        under the chinaberry tree.

For years they heard her tell it
        and always the very same
Until they avoided going near her shack
        and one day smelled her dead
They buried her at the edge of a wood
        had to dig through roots to go deep
Then said a few quiet words
        and ran shouting back inside their fence.

Shroud

Born in better times, the boy
      tiptoed to a windowed world
Then ran outside into the sun
      ate the fields and drank the streams
Holding hard to the mix of things
      and rising early to more distant views
Stood to enfold it all as his domain
      in the honing of humble miracles
He may have magnetized the world
      a savior with the right resolve
Making of this munificent place
      a monument to moral right
In finding the brilliant balm
      to salve the hurting hordes
But no, that year when he was eight
      for failure of one rain to come
At just the right time and place
      there in the lower forty
The father kicked the dust and moved
      the remnants of his make-piece life
To wetter fields but fallow grounds
      for the blank and gazing boy

Who failed to fit the balance now
        and melted in to measured paths
Laid out for him by formula
        to normalize his nomad life
And so matured in mediocrity
        he moved a million miles away
Well out of place and out of time
        to comfort and conspired habit
His wife and oatmeal children
        moving too from hand to mouth
And hating him for failed promise
        that they felt but could not know
And so he died at fifty-six
        beset with weeds and rain
With no more than a passing thought
        on the lazy waste of things.

Abandoned house, Highway 3

Condo Coming

The tiniest beetle under
      the briefest scrap of leaf
Starved to death last night
      in the middle of this forty prime acres
Searching for the tree
      it was born to climb and chew
And find its seasonal mate to procreate
      its humble number in cyclic union

The fragile shell empties of its
      last particles of protein
As microscopic mites devour the remains
      fighting in desperate hordes
Leaving their epic numbers destitute
      dead and dying in turn
Enriching the soil with organic death
      laid desolate for sterile parking space

Thus made bugless, the plot
      is squared and cordoned off
And swarmed by moiling minions
      who plant geometric trees

Of the wrong flavor
    mocking the unity of the waiting wood
Where beetles thrive and blood abounds
        among the unplanned multitudes

New-ground near Woodward

A bloodless coup now holds
        encroaching dominion
For those who count up their collection
        of sweat and blood and tears
And swap it for a unit
        of manufactured dreams
With guarded gate and parking space
        and full fumigation services
    Shrieking at an occasional dying beetle
        snipping vines and weeds with vengeance
Consigning scraps of leaves
        to compost for the starving trees
Here at the carefree flattened world
        of wonderful Dominion Hills.

The Simple Life

Marlene was in Paris
When *Blue Angel* played here
And Ezra and Mollie sat holding hands
Thinking of the hands more than the movie
While Marlene sat bored at the Sorbonne
Hearing an Italian stud's
Fractured French
Try to conjugate its way
Into her britches

They stopped at a half-filled cotton shed
On the way back home and did it
Pushing and pulling at each other
While Marlene in wine-heavy distraction
Watched the stud in a half-empty room
Act like a diplomat.

Abandoned movie theatre, Blackville

Cenotaph

Well, hell, I'm forgotten
          my 63 years nothing
All that worry and crap
          amounting to this:
A jaybird's fart in a
          wild cherry tree
Oh, I loved to strut
          in my clean khakis
And be good and do right
          in everybody's eyes
My conscience and I
          staying on the best of terms
Letting things happen
          and fall where they would
Enjoying the experience
          and missing the meaning

I loved both wisely and well
          warming some, scorching a few
Who touched me but never consumed
          I was occasionally tasted
And, like a bull at a cowlick

lingered once or twice at the salt
Few pretty days were wasted on me
    the simple things soaking in
Absorbed into my comfortable soul
    like the horizon, the setting sun

Isolated woodside grave, Highway 394

Until it turned on me one
    day and started oozing out instead
But even then, corpulent with memories
    replete with subtle exercises and triumphs
I hitched my belt tighter against the insipid flow
    and smiled at the multitudes
And in my many missions knew:

They'll remember me forever!
Now they have taken my life
        totally out of context

Who could forget my subtle sacrifice
        for the sake of Mamie's children
The pain I showed the world
        when my own daddy died
The remark I made about the weather
        the season everybody suffered?
Now even the jaybird's flown
        and its fetid sibilance faded
I would take the worms back
        Life! Life! Any form or fashion. Please!

These mineral strips where my bones once lay
        no longer have connection
I have fallen from memory
        of all living things
Even my meager hieroglyphs
        marking my birth and death
Reduced to smooth sameness
        by pulsating rain and sun
And I yearn for the feel
        of the unified flow
Let me rejoin, touch the ebb
        and begin to move once more!
Am I alone in this among my mineral peers
Who lie in well-marked graves
        in fenced and weather-free rows
Devoid of trees and farting birds

and serendipitous discovery in the wild?
Yes, hell. But I have a head start of them
        at rejoining the ebb and flow
That little tree off to my left
        is ready to assert itself this spring
And into my vital boneyard
        the tiniest tendril of root will creep
Probing, testing, tasting. Tasting!
        And into that moving wonder
I will be entrenched and flow
    and never stop again, I know.

The Armadillo Waltz

Everybody lives down the road
Just about half a mile from Mama
And won't let you forget it
In this self-congratulatory state
Electrically alive to the imagined slight
And somnambulant under noonday light

They do the armadillo waltz here
       dancing like costumed gods
With practiced grace and
       feigned countenance
They bow and smile and
       glide in circles
One behind the other
       repeating the steps and repeating the steps
Wallowing in the boredom of perfection

And in the finest restaurants here
As in their churches too
They dress their best and pray to impress
As they order and eat the menu

Replete and complete with yesteryear
And inoculated against future shock
They manhandle today
Beat it in the face with a tire tool

That glorious time
          when the pope came
They marveled at the motorcade
          got mired in the meaning
And mostly mocked his infallibility
          as they assumed the first position
And waltzed away in laughter

And on Billy Graham's ride into town
They spoke in tongues
          up close and tight
Babbling about Brooks Brothers suits
          and the cast of the hem of his garment
Filling his coffers with bales of greenbacks
          spent on journalistic thank yous
Bought and paid for sanctimony
          and reviled Jim and Tammy, who kept it all
Who boogied when they should have waltzed
          in the ultimate superiority
Of the free over those found guilty
          of poor public relations
As they stem the tide
          in their tidy steps
In tight correct circles
          there in the State House halls
Where pomp and circumstance reign supreme

and stentorian calumny abounds
And the armadillo waltz is the catalyst
that brings it all around.

State Capitol Building

The Dresser

I used to put on my britches
One leg at a time
Till I was elected and *lo!*
Now all I have to do is
Think pants and they're on me
Like white on rice
It's wonderful good the little things
That come with the suit
I stroll among the hired hands
And keep the requisite distance
The pleats of my trousers
Sharp enough to cut a swath
Through their simple ranks

Governor's Mansion

But I've got my eye pressed
On a wider path
Snipping out a niche in history
Where the fold of your fabric
Is carved in stone, falling full
With glory and fame
And lasting forever, my fellow citizens
(But let that pass for now)

For the moment, I square my shoulders
Tuck in my shirttail
And fit today to the pattern
To sew up that neat majority
At base a simple stitch in time

To thread my way into the mind
Of every manqué mannequin I meet
Plus, a kerchief for a fashion plate
To throw the weight my way
And thus, will I be forever clothed in gold
But till that time
I stitch every single moment by hand
Very carefully
And for now must mount
A pair of plastic collar stays
Against the omnipresent wrinkle

The midnight media asked me once
To tell my private wish
Strictly on the sly, they said
But I know sly, since sly I am
And thus, plated my tongue in silver
Spake of happiness wrapped in flags
And then they backed off so far
I feared a bit they'd not come back
But they always do in case I trip
And rip a hem or pop a golden thread
But in the quiet while they were gone
I cupped my wishes in my hand
Gazed into the crystal mists at my miracle land
And sighed to see myself, bereft of raiment there
In meadows, mingling with the milling crowds
Naked and gleaming in the sun
Strolling quietly among the unclothed multitudes
Smiling and clasping hands in green pastures
With trees and shade and rolling hills

And streams anointing tender limbs
The people perfect in every way
And there without a word or thought
They form a line and wait their turn
To love me, one by one, on hidden grassy slopes.

Committing Art

We codify feelings here
And subsidize them
In warm benevolence
With efficient grants
And feel-good business

See our procedures?
They come in triplicate
With consistency, sequence
Hierarchy, and condescension
See our geometric building?
It expresses us and our mind-set
As we assume our public posture
Of committing art

We scurry about its
Halls and walls, and angle-space
Tucking bits of paper here
Smoothing stacks of effluvia there
And acknowledging with practiced humility
The homage from recipients of our largess

We honor those whose talent
Is malleable
Yielding to our forms
And yearning for pre-conception
And lots of mutual admiration

We spend most of our
Nine-to-five lives
In the lotus-laden land
Between the wish and fulfillment

Art is all.

State Arts Commission

Solitaire: War Memorial

Death comes along just once, you know
At base a simple thing:
The failure of one breath to catch
And hold the knotted string

It does not come along in hordes
It does not come in waves
It cuts just one breath at a time
In solitary phase

Discount the mournful numbers here
And contemplate each name
Reject the abstract tragedy
Uproot the seeds of blame

Viet Nam Memorial, Columbia

Instead erase each name in turn
Then write it back in place
And in the interim regard
The difference that it made:

A love untouched, an unborn child
An empty room at home
A season's worth of life still furled
A past and future gone

Beware those who would count the lines
And speak of numbers here
The tragedy is in the man
And not the hemisphere

War does not care, it cannot feel
So speak in concrete terms:
Who stopped this one breath laid in stone
And strangled its return?

Death comes along just once, you know
At base a simple thing:
The failure of one breath to catch
And hold the knotted string

It does not come along in hordes
It does not come in waves
It cuts just one breath at a time
In solitary phase.

Sanctum

We never have been able
To get it quite right in our mind
Whether it was Jesus or Lord
That was God
But whoever or whichever
It rested on Sunday
So we chose Saturday for God's sake
What difference does it make
We're resting in his name, you know
See these scholarships?
We've stacked them heaven-high
So poor starving kids can come
And be converted to the way

Parking space does not come cheap
But it's the cross we bear
To light another library shelf
And put a runner on the stair
We congregate at our tailgate
And pass communion there
Soaked in spirit and salvation
The Lord drank wine, you know

Or Jesus did if he's the one
It wasn't grape Kool-Aid

Football Stadium, University of South Carolina

See our shouting multitudes
Awash in ritual light
We honor each bloody sacrifice
And bow before our saints
At play on the turf of the Lord
Running a tight end for Jesus
Praise him! Praise him! See that pass?
Over the heads of the unready
It sails through the big, blue dome
In divine deliverance to outstretched arms
We fall in homage to the chicken
Our prayers against the dog

Deliver us from the tiger
The ram, the eagle, and the lion

We are all sheep, you know
Our mutton chops turned into jowl
As we rest and bleat in ceremony
From pyramid pew piled upon pew
It is on this holy solid rock
We have made our father's house
That all our godly work goes on
In our Sabbath state of mind.

Semantic Interstices

A cheap shot as a symbol
The house is mostly garage
Slung in nondescript sprawl
Among the usual trees
But ah the lake!
Manmade and picturesque
Efficient and controlled
A pooled mirror of the heavens
And mountain crags and storms at sea
Given Dickey's distant gaze

He stands on the dock
Fashioning a fine linguistic net
And casts a wary knowing eye
At the multitudes awash in the ripples
Who splash about their day
And hardly notice
Until he tries a fling
And froths the surface
The tender threads he has knotted
In painful proportions
Probing now beneath the surface

In subtle search for meaning there
Goddamn you all! he cries aloud
I'll drain this hellhole swamp, you know!
And while the lake is still as stone
He sheds his clothes and shows his skin
A great white vision of a whale
He takes his fish knife as always
And pricks himself in private parts
Then flicks a drop of steaming blood
Onto the silent surface, awaiting signs

James Dickey's house, Lake Katherine

He cleanly cuts a deeper slice
And chucks it at the opposite shore
Oysters will do, he tells the depths
I mean Hemingway couldn't eat

The one he caught and choked and drowned
And down he slices with the blade
Deeper this time and into bone
Scraping until the very marrow
Seeps out and coagulates

And still the silent water stares
As shadows creep across its face
The sun as always sets again
And leaves him there a bloody mess
Empty and starving another day
In darkness then, he resurrects
And quietly wades across the lake
The shallow shoals he knows by heart
And sloshes through the minnowed pools
Consigned to circling circumstance
Returns to where he first began
To start another net at dawn.

How Religions Start: The Trinity

The Mother

I afford jonquils in December
Brad being a lawyer and all
That goes with it
Porcelain in our entryway
Three cars and a boat
A dirt bike and electric carving knife
My truncated days adrift
So I can go with the flow
Brunches and all, you know
But no spring picnic either
That disaster last April

When Janelle asked me the time
And my Rolex had stopped!
I froze at the pause that filled
All kinds of time for me
Are you sure that's a Rolex, dear?
Looks like to me it has two i's.

Now Brad is taking to drink
And my son to toking pot
While I bust my oversized butt
At PTA and women's leagues
And try to keep it all together
Thank God for church
I mean that literally
And not in sacrilegious idiom
Having failed to win cheerleader
As a popular sophomore
And becoming a mainstay
of the junior league

I have survived if not prevailed
And now seek the solace
Of that Sabbath sanctuary
Where I know my lines
And every movement by heart
My sacred pew is the one place
Where I can take it all to rest
Leaving it to the vicar
To lead us down those cushioned ruts
Where way leads on to way
And our collective minds can coast
Give me the rituals of life
And I can do without the realities.

The Son

My mind's not tired, you know
Just heavy and needing to sprint

To some meaning and measure it
Against the size of my birth announcement
Not the oatmeal they serve on Sunday
All slimy hot or gummy cold

Give me the sun outside the narthex
Not Captain Midnight in the pulpit
Out here, I feel the truth
Like seed beneath the surface
Waiting for sunlit solutions
To burst forth on the waiting world
The closest I think I've ever come
To making the seeds connect
Is occasional Keats or Shelley
Moving in a crystal moment
Inside the kingdom of the cloud-god

Oh, leave me here and let it last!
I don't want to go to church
To hear a manufactured minister
Tell a microphone about the building fund
I sicken at the sound of rote and rite
Bouncing off colored windowpanes
And soaking into the seamless rug
Amid this world of weather-free worship

Let me take over the church
I will renew the original promise
Turned now to makeshift memory
And manifested mostly in ornate things
I will chase the slouching beast

From its thrall of Bethlehem
My time come around at last, I will do it all again:
Smash the windows and flail the floor
Burn the images and unlock the door
Sprinkle dirt upon the sparkling congregation
And plant a seed in the rotting carpet.

The Father

In case you do not know the word for me
Let me tell you here and now: *cuckold*
Why don't they say it out? I'm nothing more
Than a shallow symbol in a chenille robe
Having failed at the inn thing
That son of mine you'd think was born whole-cloth
Unto my wife everything, she remaining virgin
In the process, for God's sake
And me forever soft and sinless
A wakeless pageant walk-on in a silent role.

Trinity Cathedral, Columbia

Desecrating the Daily News: Noblesse Oblige

Anointing this state with news
>is like feeding cotton candy to a child
Who vomits on you
>and looks to you to wipe its chin
Our hands are clean
>untouched and untied
As we maintain our fourth estate
>with gates and guards and broad surveys

Being first is tough, they say
>we do not know and do not care
Being *only* is tougher still
>but it's the cross we wear
Monopoly hangs above us
>like a soft billowy cloud
Whereupon we rest our heads
>and lead paragraphs
And keep a snuggling vigil
>from the comfort of our pillow
Like a child watching a storm
>from a weatherproof room

We wet our finger in the wind
        and hold it west and north again
Then measure news in coffee spoons
        and research the need for more cartoons
The biggest pages in the state
        that money buys and webs collate

It's no easy task. At times
        the AP stream is flat and UPI is out
That's when we set records for Public Service
      especially those who count their lines

But all's not bread and roses here
        we sally forth on one-way streets
And save our most acidic ink
        for mediocre restaurants
How dare they plop within our realm
      and not expect a sneak attack
All is food in love and war
        our night-shift cynics want to say
They fear us like the plague they are
        unless of course they advertise

With careful steps we walk the row
        and pluck what others cared to sow
Our rights are circumscribed on high
        and though our voice won't stem the tide
Our echo cannot be denied.

File

Many a macrobiotic mind
       has come to rest here
Finding comfort among the memos
       and safety in recycling
Papered nests of tufted neologisms
       abound, begetting progeny
Leading on to circumstance
       and biodegradable deeds
While securely at a distance
       the source goes fitfully on
The classroom generator, underfed
       and overrun with heat and light
Its current coming from the probe
       of little questions, big replies
Feeling for the fickle spark
       to free the pressure, break the bind
Releasing clouds and wild accord
       to stoke the distant duplicators

State Department of Education, Columbia

Who sit in bureaucratic splendor
      measuring their mediocrity
In coffee spoons by Prufrock
and situations by Sanka
A dwelling whose role implies
      the mightiest of minds
And mellowest of reason and romance
      should dwell here
Belies its logic. Afloat in hierarchy
      and sequence, it files away its name.

Fundamentalist television station, West Columbia

Preacherman

Bending low over my campfire
I heard the voice of God
Rolling across the manmade lake
Where I knelt in humble prayer and heard
Of all the choices the world around
I'll take you to spread my word
To the four corners of this flat earth
My word being what you choose
Amen and was gone, thus said-ith the Lord
Whose tongue, more normally bent
Toward the pastoral tone of King James
Spoke in more workaday idiom to me
Which I understood verily and went forth

But first stopped by my double-wide
Fell to my knees, beseeching Myrtis for forgiveness
So that she took me back again and told the kids
To go out and play, their daddy was back home
And thus delivered, I awaited revelation
How best to preach the loving word of God

And landed on the medium of television
Medium meaning between high and low
And hitting the great in-between of humanity
Perfection leading on to holiness, with practice helping
I sought at large, a plugged-in pulpit
But finding none for rent right then and feverish to manifest
The sacred words in focus on the camera of my mind
I seized last Christmas's bonus toaster
And, for practice in a staging presence
Implored its mirrored metal mind
To repent, to hear the mind of God
To seek deep within its shiny soul
And come to wash in the warm bread of Jesus
Reciting bible verse and phrase, I warmed
The kitchen with brimstone energy
Commanding that make-piece metal eye
To deliver the words of manna manifold
As Myrtis trembled and came in ecstasy
The bread popping out brown and crunchy
Seared by the sweat of my sacred song

I knew I had the market made
And thus, left her high and dry
Again, and went across the land
Spreading the word like mayonnaise
On Southern bread, thick and rich
And reaching multitudes in need

So that now I bend low
Over my poolside barbecue
And give the word of God

Where and how I choose
Having a monopoly on that mighty tongue
And jostle forth in my private jet
Holy-holy-holl-i-me-o-shondai!
Saving gall bladders and ingrown toenails
The same as cancer and constipation
The price of salvation, a small amount
Multiplied a million times
Thus, do I dwell in my deliverance?
God is good as I am good, and I am
God.
Amen.

Soul Shack

You perch adroitly along the sidewalk
Facing a technically superior carwash
So salvation is working both sides of the street
Spray and dip, pray and tip
The cleansing goes on and on
Cars lined up and souls all bunched
The filth! The dirt! The layers loosed
Laid out and laundered in lye and brimstone
Till, squeaky clean and redeemed
The bodies sally forth into the sun
Until next time

House of worship, downtown Columbia

How many souls can you hold, shack?
Cathedrals are bigger, you know
And therefore closer to God
Their multitudes streaming in and out
From soaring sites and high hallowed halls
With choirs dwarfing your mingling groups
Who lean against your listing walls
And get down to dirt-based dogma

The car wash handles one at a time
And prays for sunny weather
But you – the only line you've ever known
Was when the one good deacon died
It was a rainy day but business was good

The plate went round and round
Its silver contents flashing on the sign
Across the street that says, *No tipping*.

Your days are numbered, little soap dispenser
The car wash has them lined up
And in the clean light of competition
Has made your site a hallowed ground
For profit-minded true believers
Eyeing your choice location there
On the right side of the street
To work more mundane miracles
Because corporate cleanliness
Is next to godliness
And the dirt they deal is real.

Bambi and Bubba: Meeting at the Hunt Club

Why the hell me
Does my carcass even hint
That I harbored a dangerous heart?
I mean, that self-anointed sonofabitch
Hid like a bear behind a tree
Even his clothes deceptively dyed
The color of November woods
To match his screwed-down mind
Intent on business that cold day
To put a chunk of screaming lead
In and through and out my chest

Forget that self-serving fiction
That my feelings froze on impact
Oh, no, my friend; it plain damned *hurt*
My feelings did not freeze in shock
Every nerve alive and grinding
It grabbed my shoulder blade
As it tore through to my heart
Where I stood nibbling bark
And crumbled it like a cracker

Then scattered its blueblood shards
Into my lungs and eyes.
The *hurt*. Oh, hell, it hurt
As long as I lived
Breath by shuddery breath
Every iota of what I was, was in agony

So blank out Bambi if you will
It was no drama or music-bound
It just plain damned *hurt*
With a hurt that went out of all sense of right
And proved to me there is no God
So I could not invoke what was not there
In my final searing seconds
Unlike the God-fearing bastard with the gun
Astride my steaming remains
Poking at my lolling tongue
Ready to blow another hole in me
If I twitched again
I didn't
Crystallized into diamond hate

When I was born in brush and wood
And lay my head on leaves
That wife-beating asshole was already fifty
For God's sake
And fat and well-fed
In a big family that called him Bubba
And never knew hunger or cold
Or even took a crap in my woods
But remained cement-safe in the suburbs

Exactly 291 miles from me
So we grew alongside the next four years
In creeping parallel

I ate flowers once when no one saw
And what you would call poetic
Was just me munching a bit of springtime
That's all I've ever done, really
Lifted my head over valley and stream
A part of the unified flow
Unlike that child abuser
Who, leaning into the cross hairs of his sight
Couldn't even shoot me straight
And gouged a deep hole oozing black
The blood-seeking bullet bludgeoned an organ
But they'll show shitface
How to carve me up
And miss my poisonous parts

He's got more fat than I ever had
The blood they smeared him with
Had just coursed past my eye
Not three minutes ago of the last three I had
And let me see a sylvan scene
So free in Faulkner's woods
But now his dream's supplanted mine
And he'll probably plop my sliced shank
Onto the kitchen table in steaks
Where whiney wife will curl her lips
And buy a half-meal less that week
Knowing the snotty kids will sneer

And talk about the wild
Flavor that ranges through my flesh
And push the plate of me away
Unfamiliar with the taste of free

My only consolation
And good enough, I guess
For one reduced to excrement
In an alien cement sewer
And that's our mothers, mine and his
He'll cry real tears and shake aloud
Three weeks from now
When she quietly dies a natural death
After 89 years
Of suckling senseless progeny
They'll plant her here in these waiting woods
And then next spring
On a silent balanced morning
When columbines bloom
Mine with straight staccato steps
Will march in dainty duty
From the bark-thick trees
In easy grace and facile light
And nibble in simple glory
The fresh rich grass on her grave.

The Lomans

I owned this state, Linda
Could go anywhere in it
And be at home
Black and White alike
My people loved me
That Ford was adored
Top to bottom and back again

They'd say, *Here comes Willy*
And sure enough, I'd arrive
We lived so well, you and I
Our home in Barnwell like fresh pie
Warm and flavored, and loved by all
Remember the time…
Remember the time…
How could they forget us so?
Surely this is not it
After the babies we'd hold
And the jokes I told
And the dresses you wore
They don't even come by anymore

Surely someone is still alive
Who will never forget the spring
We met and the world shifted
And made a whole new track
Just for us to follow, you and me
Unique in love and lust, girl
No one ever filled more life
Or more wholesale soap orders

Neglected cemetery near Neeses

I stocked this state in cleanliness
At every crossroads, station, and store
And now must face the dust

Of neglect for all the wholesale good
I did. My God, girl, we lasted
No longer than the soap I sold.

Tadpoles

You don't ever plan
To do junk for life
It drifts upon you
Like a river rising
When you're asleep after a long rain
You wake up
And here you are
The flotsam has floated in
And come to rest
Amid the croaking outside my window
And I looked up one day
To find I deal in junk

Somebody off somewhere said
J.C.'s got that part
Of that wrecked Rambler
In your backyard
Now my whole world
Is one backyard

Give me your tired and weary
Who live and buy for the moment

Wholesale the hell out of life
And, like a frog laying eggs
Leave a sticky stream of gook behind
A rich trail from their own guts
Hoping, through obscene proliferation
To effect a simple immortality

Surely out of all this, they tell themselves
Something will last
It doesn't, but I do
Mucking here at water's edge
Amid dried after birth and death
Dealing in detritus neither fish nor fowl.

Junkyard near Aiken

Resurrection

Like old prayers
Disregarded by God
But not forgotten by those who prayed
In the first place
We've kept the old
And built anew
Who says you can't have it all?
In side-by-side belief
Like pages from the Good Book itself
We have built here on this rock
And built again, just in case
Way does lead on to way

I mean, if the Good Book says
The man was swallowed by a fish
And while he was in there, wrote an ode
Then that's the word and that's enough
For us for it was handed down
And does not mention sanctuary
For idle smiles or random thoughts
About digestive glands or watts of light
It takes to write an ode anyplace

Those things we try to nail down first
And pray about what's left in time
The older ones can quote the ode

The deacons raised their hands to vote
To keep the old and build the new
Which stands beside in columned strength
Its classic lines a call to arms
Of the New Book's every loving line

New/Old churches near Cross Anchor

I mean if it was good enough for Jesus
It could only be good for us
Its steeple sharp and straight
Like an efficient needle
Sewing up heaven for us
And over here, we tread lightly
Over miracles and now and then
Hint among our humility

That Jonah still whispers through the cracks
Of that heavyweight steeple next door
When the winds blow and the rains flow
And we stand safely on both tracks.

Visitors

While we played dominoes back then
Old Hannah would come to this store
Smelling like the nickels she spent
On pocket cans of dark brown snuff
But never dipped in our presence
Mostly a black, humble spirit
Encircled with an off-white shawl
Dependable and consistent
Smiling with ample bosoms
The perfect social equation for us:
One nickel for one can of snuff
That only cost us one and a half cents wholesale

One day, a Yankee
In a trim straw hat
Was drinking a Grapette
When she appeared
And about went crazy
Over her and said
She was Eudora Welty's child
Whoever that was
Taken her picture with a big kodak

And used words to her
Hannah didn't know or us either
And left
All smiles and beatific

They say her picture was printed
Black and white
In a liberal magazine
But we never saw it
And probably Hannah neither
Not that it mattered, she never came back
Her grandchildren said
She was so basic
Her calico cat Tilda
Would bring in dead mice
And drop them at her feet.

Abandoned crossroads grocery near Barnwell

Down the Hard Road Apiece

So long as there's the South
There is defeat
We grow up wading through it like a lake
Whose source is drying into mud
Our steps go slower as we slough
The thick miasma of the swamp
We breathe it, cough it, hock its core
Like Thomas Wolfe, so sick with fate
Rheumatic in our fevered thought
Alive to every fancied slight
For who and what we say we are

So certain is our sense of things
Our rectitude, our coats of arms
There was a time a myth ago
When, like bent old women's silent stare
We bowed and entered a secret place
And there were taught to sing and dance
With soft-sung songs and notes so high
That only ears tuned to defeat
Could hear and reconcile the beat
Its soaring sinful cry of guilt

Its careless touch, its corrupt care
Its mottled peeks at private parts
To step, to sway, to turn, and slide
And laugh and bend the neck! But no
Our dance is dead, its memory lives
Where all our thoughts make haste to hide

State Museum in Columbia

Only here can you profess a place
Where else could carrion thought appeal
To minds at work on sanctioned deals
Alive to lazy intellect
Of moss on bricks and plexiglass
A hoary meeting of the minds
In covens of the lower class
Grown rank with fetid afterthoughts

And blank reminders of the past
Beyond this place or winks and smirks
Looms but the glory of the shade
Wherein we fashion dirty works
Wherein we smile and ply our trade.

Glass Fire

You'd never know we're lush and green
And blush unseen or love our best out on the grass
Beyond the road and from the light

In softer hours, we blend our ways
Our shadows curve and press the flesh
That tastes of mint and fresh lymphatic growing things

It's at our worst when you are here
And gaze upon our stalks and limbs
A judgment call against our dry and empty leaves

Junk car orchard near Summerville

But oh, when you have turned away
This emerald dome grows full and flows
To moiling waters you can't know

A fulsome wave, a laden tide
A mother's body, deep and wide
One angle from our looking glass.

Epilogue:
The State Beheld

Where roses grow in saffron light
     and soft-sung insects sail the air
Where shocks of birdsong pierce the quiet
     and languid leaves caress the rain
Where softest skies enfold the clouds
     and secret streams anoint the land
Where unseen music fills the mind
     and life secretes lymphatic days
Where fertile fields invite the meek
     and softness cushions every floor
Where warming winds perfume the walks
     and spirits are made manifest

There rapists thrive on innocence
     and richness lives in poverty
There mayhem marks the garden path
     and lazy minds turn into thieves
There child abusers stroll the malls
     and alcoholics drink and pray
There painful pasts are born again
     and preachers prey on ignorance

There condos stack like children's blocks
		and every inch of beach is stayed
There beauty turns upon itself
		and conscience takes a distant view

Herein are buried better ways
		when sanctimony comes and stays
Herein resides the paraphrase
		when good ole boys come out to play.